KEYS TO WALKING IN PERSONAL VICTORY

The Battle Is Not Yours, But God's.

MORRIS CERULLO

Published by:
MORRIS CERULLO WORLD EVANGELISM
P.O. Box 85277 • San Diego, CA 92186
(858) 277-2200
E-mail: morriscerullo@mcwe.com
Website: www.mcwe.com
For prayer, call: (858)HELPLINE
E-mail: HELPLINE@mcwe.com

MORRIS CERULLO WORLD EVANGELISM OF CANADA
P.O. Box 3600 • Concord, Ontario L4K-1B6
(905) 669-1788

MORRIS CERULLO WORLD EVANGELISM OF GREAT BRITAIN
P.O. Box 277 • Hemel Hempstead, HERTS HP2-7DH
+(0)1 442 232432

TABLE OF CONTENTS

INTRODUCTION

We serve a great God! Do you believe that God speaks to people today? The Father spoke to me. He said to me, "Son, I am going to touch the circumstances of my people." Will you be honest with God – and you know that it doesn't pay to be dishonest with Him anyway, right? Because God knows our mind. He knows our heart. Sometimes God just likes us to tell Him how much we need Him. Isn't that right?

Are you facing a personal circumstance...a personal problem...in your life, in your family, with your children – some personal need that you have? Have you been in conflict with the power of the enemy? Well, the Father has told me to tell you that He is going to come into that circumstance in your life!

When I was almost 15, God came to me in a Jewish Orthodox orphanage. I had no father; I had no mother. I had gone through the rituals of seven years of Hebrew school. I was bar mitzvahed. At that time, God came into that Jewish Orthodox orphanage and brought me the message that Jesus Christ is the Messiah.

When I was 15, God took me from this earth and brought me into the heavens to stand before His revealed presence. In that experience God asked me for my life, and I gave it to Him.

Then, after I turned 16 and had already been out preaching, one day I was in a wooded area in the mountains of northern, upstate New York. I can see it as if it were today. I was on my knees praying, asking God – a little boy called to the nations of the world – "How can I help Your people?"

And, the Father said to me, "Son, take out your pen and write." He said, "I'm going to give to you a revelation for My people. If they will follow what I am about to tell you, they will never experience unanswered prayer. My people will have 100 percent victory, 100 percent of the time, over 100 percent of the enemy.

This book contains this revelation for personal victory that God gave me. I have good news for you! It is God's will and His desire to answer your every prayer and fulfill your every need.

If you will follow these steps, you will experience a new confidence that God has not forsaken you! This revelation message will put into your spirit a new foundation...one that will never leave you and will give you a divine ability, in the Holy Spirit, to know that God hears and answers your prayers!

God's servant,

Brother Srnulla

5

CHAPTER ONE:
THE GOD WHO ANSWERS YOUR PRAYER

The Bible says,

> *Ye shall know the truth and the truth shall make you free.*
>
> John 8:32

We are not going to sweep the problem of unanswered prayer under the carpet, nor turn our backs on it. We need not fear or make excuses...we just need to understand the truth.

The truths presented in this revelation message are so closely tied to your reading and understanding the Word of God that I am including the entire text of the Scripture for you...(II Chronicles 20:1-30).

As you read this message, remember that you are reading for a definite purpose. Even if you picked up the book by apparent accident, or if a friend gave it to you, the Holy Spirit has a definite purpose in it for your life.

Nothing in life happens by chance; God has no accidents! Jesus said, *"No man can come to me, except the Father which hath sent me draw him"* (John 6:44). We often apply this to the unbeliever, but I believe that the "coming to Jesus" this verse refers to is a continuous experience in our Christian life. And each time we are drawn closer to His presence, it is for a special God-given purpose that the Father has for our lives.

The fact that you are holding this book in your hand is a good sign that the Holy Spirit of the living God is at work in your life.

I guarantee this to you, that after receiving what the Holy Spirit has to give you through this revelation, your life will never be the same again.

This message is simple and easy to understand; and most importantly, it is easy to begin to apply to the problems that confront you every day of your life.

Read and reread this message until you have it committed to memory.

"WHATSOEVER THINGS YE DESIRE"

Just about everything that we receive from our Heavenly Father both in the natural and spiritual worlds is based upon our desires. We have to really desire victorious Christian living or it will never be ours.

When we are sick, we really have to have the desire to be healed or divine supernatural forces will not be put into action on our behalf.

When we are living a defeated, compromising, powerless Christian life, we have to honestly desire the better life that Christ can give us or it will never come.

When we have unsaved loved ones, whether it be children, husband, or wife, we have to desire their salvation from the very depths of our being before spiritual forces are set in motion that will change the course of their lives, their thinking, their spiritual insight, and bring them to Christ.

Wishful thinking is not enough. *"The effectual fervent prayer of a righteous man availeth much"* (James 5:16).

Fervent to me speaks of heat, like white heat – the heat of a flame, something that is moving and comes from the innermost depths. Fervent prayer is not just some form or ritual that you mechanically go through.

Remember this, God wants you to have complete victory in your life. So many people are consumed with the belief that something they are going through – which is causing them to lose the victory in their life – is God's will. They think that it just isn't their time to live in the power of the Holy Spirit and have victory in their lives.

This is simply not true!

There just isn't any such thing!

God sent his Son into the world that He might destroy the works of the devil.

> *For this purpose the Son of God was manifested,*
> *that he might destroy the works of the devil.*
>
> I John 3:8

Jesus died that you might have the victory in your body, in your soul, and in your spirit. Don't let the devil ever put the suggestion in your mind that you are suffering and defeated because it is the will of God for your life.

The victory that I am talking about applies to the greatest crises in our lives, and may be the very reason the Holy Spirit has placed this book in your hands. This formula for victory will work for you right now! It will give you the ability to begin to apply the Word of God today which will bring the victory you need regardless how great the problem is you are facing.

Even more important for you, this revelation of the Holy Spirit will apply to your day-by-day walk through life and all of its little problems. Most great crises are the result of a buildup of a lot of little things…crises are the explosions that finally take place as a result of the day-to-day pressures that are not faced squarely and eliminated.

If the day-to-day items of conflict were handled on a day-to-day basis, even if a crisis did come that appeared to be totally beyond our control, we would have the power within us not only to cope, but to overcome and to be more than a conqueror through Jesus Christ.

In this context, this revelation applies to every born-again Christian. Remember, the Scripture says that it is the little foxes that spoil the vine – those little sly foxes that we let go by, cover over, sweep under the spiritual rug, and try to forget about them. They drain us of the spiritual power that we should be using, not only to keep the victory in our own lives, but also for spiritual warfare on behalf of others. May the eyes of your understanding be enlightened as you read this powerful portion of God's Word, from which this revelation comes:

II Chronicles 20:1-30:

> *1 It came to pass after this also, that the children of Moab, and the children of Ammon, and with them other beside the Ammonites, came against Jehoshaphat to battle.*

9

2 Then there came some that told Jehoshaphat, saying, There cometh a great multitude against thee from beyond the sea on this side Syria; and, behold, they be in Hazazontamar, which is Engedi.

3 And Jehoshaphat feared, and set himself to seek the LORD, and proclaimed a fast throughout all Judah.

4 And Judah gathered themselves together, to ask help of the LORD: even out of all the cities of Judah they came to seek the LORD.

5 And Jehoshaphat stood in the congregation of Judah and Jerusalem, in the house of the LORD, before the new court,

6 And said, O LORD God of our fathers, art not thou God in heaven? and rulest not thou over all the kingdoms of the heathen? and in thine hand is there not power and might, so that none is able to withstand thee?

7 Art not thou our God, who didst drive out the inhabitants of this land before thy people Israel, and gavest it to the seed of Abraham thy friend for ever?

8 And they dwelt therein, and have built thee a sanctuary therein for thy name, saying,

9 If, when evil cometh upon us, as the sword, judgment, or pestilence, or famine, we stand before this house, and in thy presence, (for thy name is in this house,) and cry unto thee in our affliction, then thou wilt hear and help.

10 And now, behold, the children of Ammon and Moab and mount Seir, whom thou wouldest not let Israel invade, when they came out of the land of Egypt, but they turned from them, and destroyed them not;

11 Behold, I say, how they reward us, to come to cast us out of thy possession, which thou hast

10

given us to inherit.

12 O our God, wilt thou not judge them? for we have no might against this great company that cometh against us; neither know we what to do: but our eyes are upon thee.

13 And all Judah stood before the LORD, with their little ones, their wives, and their children.

14 Then upon Jahaziel the son of Zechariah, the son of Benaiah, the son of Jeiel, the son of Mattaniah, a Levite of the sons of Asaph, came the Spirit of the LORD in the midst of the congregation;

15 And he said, Hearken ye, all Judah, and ye inhabitants of Jerusalem, and thou king Jehoshaphat, Thus saith the LORD unto you, Be not afraid nor dismayed by reason of this great multitude; for the battle is not yours, but God's.

16 To morrow go ye down against them: behold, they come up by the cliff of Ziz; and ye shall find them at the end of the brook, before the wilderness of Jeruel.

17 Ye shall not need to fight in this battle: set yourselves, stand ye still, and see the salvation of the LORD with you, O Judah and Jerusalem: fear not, nor be dismayed; to morrow go out against them: for the LORD will be with you.

18 And Jehoshaphat bowed his head with his face to the ground: and all Judah and the inhabitants of Jerusalem fell before the LORD, worshipping the LORD.

19 And the Levites, of the children of the Kohathites, and of the children of the Korhites, stood up to praise the LORD God of Israel with a loud voice on high.

20 And they rose early in the morning, and went forth into the wilderness of Tekoa: and as they went forth, Jehoshaphat stood and said, Hear me, O Judah, and ye inhabitants of Jerusalem; Believe in the LORD your God, so shall ye be established; believe his prophets, so shall ye prosper.

21 And when he had consulted with the people, he appointed singers unto the LORD, and that should praise the beauty of holiness, as they went out before the army, and to say, Praise the LORD; for his mercy endureth for ever.

22 And when they began to sing and to praise, the LORD set ambushments against the children of Ammon, Moab, and mount Seir, which were come against Judah; and they were smitten.

23 For the children of Ammon and Moab stood up against the inhabitants of mount Seir, utterly to slay and destroy them: and when they had made an end of the inhabitants of Seir, every one helped to destroy another.

24 And when Judah came toward the watch tower in the wilderness, they looked unto the multitude, and, behold, they were dead bodies fallen to the earth, and none escaped.

25 And when Jehoshaphat and his people came to take away the spoil of them, they found among them in abundance both riches with the dead bodies, and precious jewels, which they stripped off for themselves, more than they could carry away: and they were three days in gathering of the spoil, it was so much.

26 And on the fourth day they assembled themselves in the valley of Berachah; for there they blessed the LORD: therefore the name of the same place was called, The valley of Berachah, unto this day.

27 Then they returned, every man of Judah and Jerusalem, and Jehoshaphat in the forefront of them, to go again to Jerusalem with joy; for the LORD had made them to rejoice over their enemies.

28 And they came to Jerusalem with psalteries and harps and trumpets unto the house of the LORD.

29 And the fear of God was on all the kingdoms of those countries, when they had heard that the LORD fought against the enemies of Israel.

30 So the realm of Jehoshaphat was quiet: for his God gave him rest round about.

This portion of Scripture could be called the "Great Power Play," because the enemies of God put on a display of unified might designed to bring fear into the hearts of the Israelites.

This same spectacle is being repeated before our very eyes every day. Satan is the master of the power play. He accomplishes this on a collective basis against the church. Sometimes when I look at the carnal programs of evangelism conducted by our churches, I feel that the world is dictating the path the church should follow far more than the Holy Spirit.

If you would stop to truly compare the methods of evangelism used by the early church in the book of Acts and the promotions employed today, you would really wonder if these two types of evangelism really represent the same faith.

I believe in utilizing every means that our technological society provides for the spreading of the Gospel to win men and women to Jesus Christ, but I also believe that the power of the Holy Spirit has to remain the foundation of every effort and must be the common denominator between us, or we are only a sounding brass or a tinkling cymbal.

What makes a person or a church body resort to carnal weapons in spiritual warfare?

It is FEAR...fear of failure, fear of being the object of ridicule, fear of being a despised minority. Fear has been stated to be man's worst enemy, and this has been proven over and over again to be true.

President Franklin Delano Roosevelt said, "The only thing

13

that we have to fear is fear itself." And, I know he's right.

Where does fear come from?

The Bible says, "Fear hath torment" (I John 4:18). We know that this type of fear does not come from God. Paul said to Timothy, *"For God hath not given us a spirit of fear; but of power, and of love, and of a sound mind"* (II Timothy 1:7).

If this kind of fear does not come from God, then it must come form Satan. In the Scripture text which we have quoted, we see that three nations, Ammon, Moab, and Mount Seir, formed a conspiracy to come against Judah to utterly wipe it out.

Intelligence information of the massive army planning to attack Judah reached Jehoshaphat, King of Judah. The first thing that happened to him was that fear struck his heart because he knew (in the natural) that his army was no match for the great numbers that were formed against him.

At this point, fear could have completely paralyzed the nation of Judah, and they could have been utterly wiped out as a nation. You know the ramifications of that result! Because the Messiah had to come from the tribe of Judah, if there were no Judah, then there could be no Jesus. There would be none that could die for the salvation of the world. As it says in the Scriptures:

> *And thou Bethlehem, in the land of Judah, art not the least among the princes of Judah; for out of thee shall come a Governor, that shall rule my people Israel.*
>
> Matthew 2:6

The immediate results of fear determine life or death, paralysis or victory for a nation or for an individual.

We could rightly change the words of President Roosevelt to read, "The only thing that we have to fear is that fear becomes an end in itself." But, even as fear can be our greatest enemy, it can become our greatest friend if we react to it in the right way.

In every truth there is the negative side and a positive side.

Did you know there is a positive side of fear? Most of us in our Christian experience think of fear as our enemy, but fear can also be a blessing in disguise. Can you accept that?

If fear drives us to our knees to begin to travail and pray with a fervency that begins to move the hand of God that moves the world, then that fear has been channeled to be a positive influence in our life. It has forced us into a closer relationship and communion with God, and therefore has worked for our good.

If fear drives us to the Word of God to seek answers from God, then that fear has accomplished a great work in our life. Sad to say, in many cases fear is the only thing that will accomplish that objective.

Some people never become interested in the baptism of the Holy Spirit until the fear of being overcome by their problem drives them to seek a deeper meaning to their spiritual experience and life.

Here is a tragic but true commentary. Some people will never seek God in a meaningful way until sickness strikes their children or their loved ones. Let polio, cancer, or heart trouble come into the family, and all of a sudden we are searching out the Word of God and books on more effectual prayer.

We may live for ourselves all our lives with little or no attention to the things of God, but when tragedy strikes and there is no human answer, then our thought and hearts are turned in fear toward God. We start recalling the preacher's messages and the admonition of our godly parents, who up until this time, we may have considered fanatic and out of touch with this generation. Into the house of God we rush with our petition, "Lord, please help me."

I pray, "God, if it takes tragedy, if it takes fear to drive people to the place of prayer, I pray that You will scare Your people like they have never been scared before."

Jesus clearly indicated that it was much better to go through this life maimed, than to have our soul cast into eternal Hell. How can anyone disagree with that? It is simply common sense.

Jehoshaphat got so filled with fear that he called a fast. What do you think would happen to our nation right now if every pastor, every denominational leader in America would be so filled with fear concerning the future that they would stand before their congregations the next Sunday and tell the people, "Whether you realize it or not we are fighting right now in a life and death struggle, and there is only one way we are going to survive. There is only one way to remain a free nation. There is only one way to avoid a holocaust and sudden destruction. The only solution is that we all immediately begin to fast and pray that God will deliver us.

Can you imagine what would happen? I don't think you can. I know I can't. I can't begin to fathom the repentance and the sweeping move of the Holy Spirit that would begin to cleanse, purge, and purify our government and religious institutions.

The Scripture declares, "Jehoshaphat feared" (v3), and when he feared he set himself to seek the face of God. Fear acted as a spur to stir him to seek the Lord.

Many people in the world would never be living for God today if there had not been a circumstance that came into their lives which caused them fear and drove them to the place of prayer. This fear was the spark to setting their spiritual life in order. Most people reading this book will fall into one of two general classifications.

One: You are currently having a crisis in your life, and you know the fear I am talking about. Very likely if it were not for this serious problem in your life, you would not even be reading this book.

The revelation in this book will show you how to channel that fear that has gripped your life, and you will be able to look back on this experience as the greatest period of growth in your life.

Two: You do not have a crisis currently in you life but you are dissatisfied. You know that you lack victory and power to live for God. Deep down in your heart,

you also realize that these deficiencies are due to compromise in various areas of your life that you know are not pleasing to God.

Though not experiencing a dramatic moment in your life, these same keys to victory will bring you into a plateau of Christian living that you never dreamed you would attain in this lifetime; they will bring an infusion of power into your life that will prevent the necessity of a crisis to steer you into God's perfect plan for your life. This spiritual formula will be a weapon in your hands to bring you deliverance for spirit, soul, and body. Prepare yourself to receive this revelation from God so you can also receive, once and for all, what you have been praying for to fulfill the needs in your life.

Put your hand on your head over your mind right now. And pray with me, "Father, I anoint this mind in the Name of Jesus. God give it a spiritual breakthrough to comprehend this revelation truth from Your Word. Take this simple but powerful message and transform it into the realities of my life to take me past head knowledge into a new experience of relationship with You. Thank you. In Jesus' Name, Amen."

VICTORY IS MINE!

Now, let us go step by step through this great experience of Jehoshaphat's prayer. First, we will discover four great steps to victory, and best of all, the knowledge that God answers prayer. In God's answer to Jehoshaphat's prayer, we will find three keys to our complete and final victory over the problems we confront.

CHAPTER TWO:
The God We Serve Has Unlimited Power

One of the great secrets of spiritual warfare is to know that nothing happens by accident. Hear me carefully. I'm going to share several keys to walking in personal victory with you, and you're going to get an awesome revelation!

When you are facing the personal circumstances and battles that you have in your life, in your family, in your relationships, with your children, or in your spiritual life – know that those battles didn't just pop up. There are two forces in this world: God, and the devil. God has not planned any defeats for you, but Satan conspires against you.

If you just take a moment to stop and think about what you are going through and where the attacks are coming from in your life, you'll recognize that those things didn't just happen by accident. There is power at the root that has been germinating that conspiracy to come against you in your life and attack you.

The first thing that happened was this conspiracy became known. If you don't know that you are in a spiritual warfare against the enemy, you will never be able to devise the right methodology for victory.

So, when the conspiracy is known – when you get the revelation and understand that what's going on in your life is not a matter of a battle with flesh and blood – you will realize it goes beyond that! At that point, you start to get prepared to be able to deal with it.

Recognize that when you pray, you are calling upon God Almighty.

> *O LORD God of our fathers, art not thou God in heaven?*
>
> II Chronicles 20:6

The first step that Jehoshaphat made toward the solution of his problem was that he fully recognized Who he was calling upon. Jehoshaphat established that the God he is calling upon is the God of heaven...the God of all creation.

Now, what is the first thing that normally happens in a battle? Fear sets in. When fear rules, you miscalculate the enemy's strength. II Chronicles 20 says in the third verse, *"As Jehoshaphat feared..."* When he feared, the Bible said, *"He set himself to seek the Lord, and he proclaimed a fast."*

So now the enemy is revealed; his plans are known; he's coming to defeat me; he's coming to destroy me; he's coming to take all of ISRAEL. Jehoshaphat gets so afraid, he calls a fast and says, "Everybody – to your knees! Pray!" And, the whole nation obeys.

If doom were hanging over our heads, the first thing we would do is cry out to God to immediately destroy our enemy or to deliver us completely from the enemy's presence.

But what did Jehoshaphat do?

The first thing he does is to get on his knees, and while everybody else is praying too, Jehoshaphat leads out in prayer. Jehoshaphat cries out, "...Oh God of our fathers, art not thou God in heaven?" Look at what he's doing. He's recognizing Who he is calling upon. When you pray, when you speak, you're not talking to the air. Do you know that when you open your mouth and begin to talk, you are talking to the Creator of heaven and earth?

The second thing he did – are you ready for this? He said, "Art not thou God that rules over all the kingdoms of the heathen, and in Thy hand is there not power and might so that none is able to withstand you?" He never told God about Ammon. He never told God about Mount Seir. He never told God about his problem. But, he came worshipping!

Jehoshaphat recognized that He to Whom he was speaking was God, and before ever explaining to Him his need, Jehoshaphat was telling God, "You know, you have so much power; you have so much might. God, You can do anything!"

The God we serve is an Unlimited God!

Go back and repeat that phrase. Say it over and over again until its mighty truth fills your being. Our God knows no limit! Jehoshaphat knew that God was able to open the Red

Sea to let the children of ISRAEL pass through. The same God fed the entire nation of ISRAEL in the wilderness for forty years.

He is the God that could send down the fire from heaven. He is the God that could cause the axe head to swim and the donkey to talk.

The false prophets could not withstand His power. God's fire consumed the offering and the altar of Elijah which was to them an open rebuke.

The lion Samson conquered could not withstand the power of God. The Philistines could not withstand His power; Jonathan and his armor bearer put them to flight.

It was His power that shielded Shadrach, Meshach, and Abednego in the fiery furnace that was heated seven times hotter than normal.

It was His power that gave the lions lockjaw as Daniel walked among them and spent the night in their den.

Sickness could not withstand His power as Jesus of Nazareth went about doing good and healing all who were oppressed of the devil. He said to the blind, "See," and the dark scales fell from their eyes.

As Jesus said to the deaf, "Hear," the sensation of sound began to register on their brains. As He said to the mute, "Speak," those paralyzed tongues were released by the power of God to begin to function for the first time.

The natural elements could not oppose the power of Jesus. As He spoke to the storm and the raging waters to be calm, they stopped their tempest without putting up a further argument. The devil could not withstand His power as He spoke to the demon-possessed and said, "Come out!" and immediately they were set free.

Jehoshaphat is saying, "God, I know You can do it. God I know You will do it. God, You will deliver Your people. You will heal me from this cancer. You will deliver me from this rheumatoid arthritis, God. You will bring my wayward, backslidden daughter back home again, God. You will save my wife, and unite our family once again."

"God, I know that it is not by might, nor by power that we can ever defeat the enemy no matter how large our armies are, nor how small the enemy's armies. Lord, You have shown ISRAEL over and over again that when they had the stronger army by numbers and in trained warriors, they were defeated if You were not fighting for them. So, "God, we know that our answers are not in numbers, but our answer is in Your power to deliver."

Think of that for a moment! Begin to apply that thinking to your crisis and all the problems that are facing you today.

It is not more money that will solve your financial problems; it is the blessing and power of God active and alive upon that which you already possess, no matter how much it is.

The answer to the healing of that cancer is not in greater or more expensive medical treatments, or drugs; it is in the delivering power of Jesus Christ.

Jehoshaphat clearly established in his own mind exactly Who he was asking for deliverance and the potential of His power.

Remember that in his hour of trial, Jehoshaphat, like a great leader, kept calm. Or, in other words as our generation would say, "He kept cool."

There is a dynamic spiritual secret of knowing how to come into God's court. Recognize that you are not coming to a man, a vessel, or an instrument that is being used by God as a channel for blessing, but to your very own Heavenly Father! He is the God Who created the heavens and the earth. You are communicating with the highest, greatest power of heaven and earth.

Think of it! God Almighty Himself. Take this first step now, and begin to put the foundation of answered prayer into place. Repeat after me:

"O God, You are God; there is no other God beside You. You are the Creator of heaven and earth, and in Your right hand there is power and might so that none is able to withstand You. There is no sickness You cannot heal. There is no problem You cannot solve. There is no power You cannot overcome.

You are God! Everything in heaven and earth is under Your power. You are above all!"

CHAPTER THREE:
A Mighty God of Spiritual and Physical Deliverance

Now, are you ready for the next step? Watch this. He says, *"Art not thou our God?"* I want you to know that our God rules and reigns! Don't forget it. God belongs to you. He's God, but He's our God! He rules the heathen, but He belongs to us. We are His people! We are His children!

Jehoshaphat said, "You drove out the inhabitants of these lands. You gave this land to us." Then it grabs onto the most important thing you and I can possibly do. It's pivotal in our prayers. It's pivotal in our relationship. It's significant to our success. Jehoshaphat said, "You said, Lord" – let's read the whole Scripture...He said:

> *7 Art not thou our God, who didst drive out the inhabitants of this land before thy people Israel, and gavest it to the seed of Abraham thy friend for ever?*
> *8 And they dwelt therein, and have built thee a sanctuary therein for thy name, saying,*
> *9 If, when evil cometh upon us, as the sword, judgment, or pestilence, or famine, we stand before this house, and in thy presence, (for thy name is in this house,) and cry unto thee in our affliction, then thou wilt hear and help.*
> 2 Chronicles 20: 7-9

Remember what God has done for you in times past. It is important that you know for yourself the records of God's deliverance in the past which are recorded in the Bible. It is important for your faith that you know how God has always delivered His people from every physical and spiritual affliction into which they have fallen.

Of equal importance is the knowledge of your personal relationship with God. Jehoshaphat recited the historical evidence that God was with ISRAEL in the past; but now, he declares that God's power and presence are not only "past tense."

God was, but always is the God of the present, the now, the immediate. God is *"a very present help in trouble"* (Psalm 46:1).

One of the greatest truths ever written in the Bible is found in the 23rd Psalm. King David said, "The Lord is my Shepherd." Here, we have personal application that God is not only God and present at the moment, but He is to David, "my Shepherd," not just any shepherd. God is a personal God.

Jehoshaphat found the secret of knowing God in a personal way. The historical connection was not good enough. Your mother, father, grandfather, sister or brother can know the Lord, but that is not good enough for you. God is declaring His relationship with you.

In Isaiah, we hear this great promise of the Lord to His people:

> *When thou passest through the waters, I will*
> *be with thee; and through rivers, they shall not*
> *overflow thee; when thou walkest through the fire,*
> *thou shalt not be burned; neither shall the flame*
> *kindle upon thee. For I am the LORD thy God, the*
> *Holy One of Israel, thy Savior; I have given Egypt*
> *as thy ransom, Ethiopia and Seba in thy stead.*
>
> Isaiah 43:2-3

Note the personal application here: "I will be with thee"… not a messenger, not someone appointed, either heavenly or earthly, but God personally will be right there in the midst of your problem to deliver you…not your brother or your sister, but you. You are the one that God will deliver in the times of trouble. The fires may rage, but if you keep your trust in God, you will never be burned; the waters may rise all around you, but God will be right there to see that they never overcome you. You will not drown.

God does not guarantee that you will not go through

tribulation such as a flood, or have trials that appear to be as a mighty, raging fire around you. You may feel the intensity of the water or the heat of the flaming fire, but the waters will not go over your head, nor will your flesh be burned.

This is the revelation: God is not only big enough to take care of the entire universe, but He is also at the same time able to care for you. He is interested in the slightest detail of your life. He is concerned about you personally. Hallelujah!

Spiritual progress is impossible without a personal relationship with God. In the Old Testament, the relationship was experienced through the symbols of the Temple and the priesthood; but today, our personal relationship with God is directly through Jesus Christ, His Son.

Before Christ, the relationship had to be through symbols because the sacrifice for sin was imperfect, and there always had to be a wall or partition, a middleman, between God and man.

But we read that now Jesus has removed the middle wall or partition, whereby we can boldly enter into the Holy of Holies where our requests and petitions are made known to God in prayer.

> *For he is our peace, who hath made both one, and hath broken down the middle wall of partition between us...*
>
> Ephesians 2:14-15

If Jehoshaphat could speak of the Lord God in such a personal way, and he only knew Him by His acts and by the symbols of the Temple and priesthood, and by the shadows of the law of Moses; how much more should our faith be lifted up to believe God for the impossible.

Now our relationship is not through an intermediary; our salvation and the remission of our sins are through the sacrifice of God's own Son, Jesus Christ.

If Jehoshaphat was able to touch God with such a prayer, we have the potential for far greater victories for the Kingdom of God. Jehoshaphat continues his prayer, "Are not thou our God, who didst drive out the inhabitants of this land before thy people ISRAEL, and gavest it to the seed of Abraham thy friend for ever?"

This is the turning point of this great prayer. Here is the transition from just the fact of Who God really was, to what the Lord God had really done. Now we are moving from the static to the active.

By remembering not only Who God was but what he had done, Jehoshaphat was moving from wishful thinking to positive action. It is one thing to wait, and another thing to move.

Your faith can grow by recounting the historical acts of God which we have already mentioned; but do not stop there. That is only the beginning.

Look at your own life and begin to recall the mighty provision of God for spiritual and physical deliverance.

Start at the point of your salvation. Stop for a moment and think about what God has saved you from and recognize the transformation that has come into your life since you have known Jesus as your personal Savior.

Can you remember something God did for you in the past...that answered prayer...that healing in your body...that financial miracle...that blessing in your home?

Begin to recall the acts of physical healing and deliverance that you personally or your own immediate family have received.

If you are a newborn Christian, and none of your family have ever had a real born-again experience; then read in the Bible the miracle stories of God's deliverance. Read what God has done in the past, but also be aware of the fact that God is still performing outstanding miracles in our day.

> *Jesus Christ is the same yesterday, and today, and for ever.*
>
> Hebrews 13:8

Although in the natural, you may not have a family

member that has had a true spiritual experience with God; you are a part of the great family of God in the earth today. When you read or hear of a miracle of healing that your brother or sister in the Lord has received, you can rejoice just as if they were your own flesh and blood relatives.

God is no respecter of persons, and what He has done for others, He will do for you in your life right now.

Don't forget for one moment that the same nail-scarred hand that was laid upon your sin-fevered brow which brought you perfect peace, the greatest miracle in all the world, is ready right now to deliver you from the problem that is troubling you today.

What God did for you in the past, He will do for you again! Remember, remember, remember what God did for you in the past and you will know what He is going to do for you in the future.

Why is there tremendous interest in the occult, and in particular, predictions of the future in the realm of psychic phenomena, fortune telling, and astrology in this present hour?

People have never been more insecure about the future. They want to know what is going to happen – good or bad. We don't need any crystal-ball gazer to tell us how to solve our problems and to tell us that the daily astrology chart is the guide of our life.

I thank God that He has given to His servants the gift of discernment of spirits, but our faith is not in discernment; our faith is not even in the gift of the word of knowledge.

Our faith stands on the Lord Jesus Christ, the Son of the living God. As we remember what He has done for us individually as a child of God, and collectively, as a member of the body of Christ, and universally as a part of the family of God, then we will know that the waters of adversity that surround us will not overflow us, nor will the fiery trials consume us.

Only when we forget or allow the clouds of trouble to blot out the mighty deliverances of God in our lives and in the

Bible are we in trouble. As we begin to take these steps the Holy Spirit will bring to our remembrance those things which He hath both spoken and done in the past.

Watch your words! Let your words agree with God's Word. Are you focused on the problem? This is spiritual suicide! Let's look at what Jehoshaphat did – or in this case DID NOT do:

Jehoshaphat still never told God about the problem. But, he took with him to the throne the words of the living God. God said, "Remind Me of my words. Remind Me of MY promises. Bring My promises before Me. Like Mary, when the angel spoke and said to her, "You're going to bear a Child." She said, "That's impossible. I don't know a man, and I'm not married, and I've never committed adultery." The angel told her how it was going to happen.

The angel said that the power of the Most High God, Mary, is going to come on you and make you pregnant.

What did she say? *"Be it unto me even as Thou has spoken it."*

God brings His words to pass. He says, *"So shall my word be that goeth forth out of my mouth: it shall not return unto me void..."* (Isaiah 55:11).

Now, he tells God that Ammon, Moab and Mount Seir are coming. Jehoshaphat then says, "God, I want You to remember something. You would not let us invade those lands. You told us to have mercy on them. And, we didn't invade them; otherwise, we'd have destroyed them. But now this is how they're coming to reward us. They have formed a conspiracy to come against us to destroy us."

This is what Jehoshaphat cries out, *"Our God, wilt thou not judge them? We have no might against this great company. Neither know we what to do. But our eyes are upon You."* They humbled themselves. They recognized that in themselves, they have no might against their enemy.

Humility is another great key to receiving the answers to your prayer and walking in victory. We will go into this in greater depth in the next chapter.

CHAPTER FOUR:
Humble Yourself and You Shall Be Exalted

Humble yourself before God and recognize your insufficiency to cope with the situation.

"...we have no might against this great company that cometh against us; neither know what we to do: but our eyes are upon thee" (II Chronicles 20:12).

The efforts of man will fail...only the power of God will prevail.

Regardless of what your need is...you have no might in yourself. You can try to think of all the things you can do in the natural. You can work out all the plans that you can devise, and they will all come to naught. What are you willing to lay before Him? Every human effort? Everything that you've tried to work out in the natural? It's not easy to surrender. Trust me. I know. If God is going to work through you, you're going to have to let go. You're going to have to turn loose. You're going to have to turn loose of that loved one – that child, that young person, that drunken husband, the immoral wife. You're going to have to turn loose of the situation.

God will work in our behalf if we give it to Him...He'll work for us if we turn it over to Him. You may say, "I don't know what to do, Lord." We're on our face before Him.

The enemy's right on top. You may be thinking, "We're going to die if You don't intervene...if You don't keep Your word. If You don't fulfill Your promise, there's no hope."

A man by the name of Jahaziel stood up in the midst of the congregation of ISRAEL and began to speak. He's a prophet, the son of Zechariah. This is what he says, "Thus saith the Lord...one more time, God. Do it again before the coming of Jesus. Anoint your servants with a heavenly anointing. Take them out of themselves, and out of their flesh, and out of their carnal minds. And, fill them, my God, with visions, with manifestations, with the words of heaven...one more time,

31

thus saith the Lord!"

This step might be the most critical step of all, for it is so hard for us to admit that we can't do it ourselves, and even more difficult to be willing to take our hands off.

Consider the greatness of this man Jehoshaphat. He was their king, the leader of the people. In their eyes he was their defender; he was their deliverer. There have been many leaders in history who would rather drag their whole nation down to defeat than to openly admit that they were not strong enough for the battle.

You have an invisible shield that is established through self-sufficiency that is very difficult for even God to penetrate. As long as you think that you have everything in hand and can fight your own battles, the Lord will let you do just that.

No doubt at this climactic moment, when Judah faced certain annihilation, Jehoshaphat remembered the words of the Lord to Solomon, his predecessor, as he dedicated this very Temple that stood before: "If my people, which are called by my name, shall humble themselves, and pray, and seek my face, and turn from their wicked ways; then will I hear from heaven, and will forgive their sin, and will heal their land" (see II Chronicles 7:14).

I am sure that the words of King David also rang in Jehoshaphat's ears, "He forgetteth not the cry of the humble" (Psalm 9:12).

As King Jeshoshaphat stood before the house of the Lord with all of his people gathered with him, he prayed, "God, I want you to know something; I am not standing here before you in my own strength. I want you to know that I completely recognize my own inability to cope with this situation. It does not take a military genius to understand that we are so outnumbered and outflanked that it is beyond human strategy, human experience or understanding to resolve."

The Scripture is very succinct, and we see the king going immediately before the people to pray; but you had better believe that there was a period of dying in the life of the king before this spirit of humility took over.

I will guarantee you that if there was any way that he could have figured out how to do it himself, he would have done it because that is human nature. We are a race of people who made the proverb, "God helps those who help themselves." This simply is not true in the Word of God.

God is teaching us to be utterly dependent on Him.

One of the biggest problems that God has with us is to wrestle the problem out of our hands. It is only when we come to the end of ourselves, and are willing to die, that we are willing to give up the reins so God can set His deliverance in motion.

One of the great missionaries of our time, E. Stanley Jones, was broken in body and spirit as a very young missionary in India. One day he prayed, "Lord you know that I am at the end of my rope."

God said to him, "IF you will give that up, I will take care of everything."

He quickly replied, "Yes, Lord, I gladly give it up to you right now." Then his ministry started, a ministry that has touched millions through his writing and preaching.

We want to hang on to something no matter how small it is. And that tiny insignificant thing can be the blockade to the power of God in your life to meet your need.

Only when we are at the end of self and are ready to die can God come in and take over. Maybe the most frequent prayer that is prayed is asking God to guide our lives. Usually we pray this most when problems start pressing in from all sides.

When you are asking for guidance from the Lord, you have to be willing to step down from the throne. As long as you are there ruling and reigning, it is impossible for God to work in your behalf.

When we ask God to lead us, but still have the reins in our own hand, we are like the parents who give his child a choice. If the child makes the right choice, the parent goes along with it; but if the child makes the wrong choice, the parent overrules. In other words, the child did not really have a choice at all.

When we ask God to help us and God directs in a way that is pleasing to us, then we will go along; but if it is contrary to our desires, then we rebel. Who is on the throne then? Of course, we are.

So many people say, "I want the will of God for my life!" What they are really saying is, "I hope that God's will for my life is the same as my will for my life."

When you are on the throne and calling the shots, so to speak, then you have to be ready to take the full responsibility for all of the results, the sicknesses, the problems, and all of the other ramifications.

We live in a highly technological world where abilities are becoming more important every day. I am speaking of specialized skills that are required in order to make a living. More and more as this age progresses, skills will become increasingly important for success in society.

This is not true of spiritual power. Your spiritual power lies solely in your ability to trust God and to throw yourself completely on Him.

Until you do this, you will not be in a position to take the three remaining steps to victory. Oftentimes when we ascend a staircase, if we are in a hurry, we may skip one or two steps; but this does not work on the spiritual staircase that God has given for power and victory in your life. Only as we place our spiritual feet firmly on one step are we prepared and qualified to move to the next step.

Most people will not put their trust completely in God as long as they feel there may be some other way out. I see them come to our crusades by the hundreds; people are "trying" God to see what will happen.

These people would be very happy if God would heal them so they would not have to go back to the doctor and incur the terrible expense of another operation, but by no means are they ready to put their trust in God completely to deliver them and lead their life for them. If it works, fine; if not, they still have something else to fall back on.

This is really the critical step. You can begin to recognize God; you can remember the things that He has done for you in the past, and you can stand upon His Word; but unless you are willing to step down and humble yourself, recognizing you own insufficiency, you will never reach the ultimate that God has for you.

This step is really not a step up, but a step down... down from the throne of self.

At this great moment in the prayer of Jehoshaphat, "self" died. If it had not been for this statement, the prayer as great as it was would simply have been a beautiful piece of oratory. Here is where he moved the hand of God. Here is where he struck the heavenly chord that God could not resist.

Jesus said, "Except a corn of wheat fall into the ground and die, it abideth alone" (John 12:24). Until death to self happens, you are on your own; God will let you work it out yourself.

Now the most important thing to learn from this step, other than the necessity of dying to self, is that you do not have to come to the very end of your rope before you give up and "let God do it."

This is what we see in the Bible. It gives us the example of men and women that came to the very end of themselves before they let God have His way in their lives.

We see what the end result is. Therefore, if we allow the Holy Spirit to really speak to our hearts, we can let go of the other possibilities right now and leave our problems completely in God's hands.

Humility does not have to wait until the end of the road when there is no way left to turn. The power of the Holy Spirit can come into your life right now and give you the power to die to self. When you get off the throne of your life, the responsibility for that physical body becomes God's, not yours.

When you get off the throne, the responsibility for choosing a life mate is no longer yours. The responsibility for that unsaved son, daughter, husband or wife is no longer yours; it becomes the Lord's responsibility.

Why?

Because "The earth is the LORD'S and the fullness thereof; the world and they that dwell therein" (Psalm 24:1).

It is all His, when you take your hands off. At the moment of total surrender it is His!

Humility is the answer!

> *The LORD is nigh unto them that are of a broken heart; and saveth such as be of a contrite spirit.*
>
> Psalm 34:18

> *...Yea, all of you be subject one to another, and be clothed with humility: for God resisteth the proud, and giveth grace to the humble. Humble yourselves therefore under the mighty hand of God, that He may exalt you in due time.*
>
> I Peter 5:5-6

What is so often prayed before God is, "Lord, make me humble." But God says, "Humble yourself."

You do not know how God will provide an answer to your prayer. But, you have no might against the cancer, that personal problem, that financial need. When you do not have the answer and there is no way out through man, you will find that God is still on the throne! He's waiting for you to humble yourself...to lean not on your own understanding...to surrender yourself. That's when you will find Him right by your side.

Right now, take this marvelous step to victory. Humble yourself before your Heavenly Father. Put all preconceived ideas, all tradition, church denominations, doctrines, and ways of man on the altar.

"Oh Lord, I have tried in myself. Now I surrender all. I have no might in myself to carry this burden, to fight this battle, to bear this pain. I am not able in myself."

In the next chapter you will discover what God does when a man comes to this realization in his life.

1 "I am the true vine, and My Father is the vinedresser.
2 Every branch in Me that does not bear fruit He takes away; and every branch that bears fruit He prunes, that it may bear more fruit.
3 You are already clean because of the word which I have spoken to you.
4 Abide in Me, and I in you. As the branch cannot bear fruit of itself, unless it abides in the vine, neither can you, unless you abide in Me.
5 "I am the vine, you are the branches. He who abides in Me, and I in him, bears much fruit; for without Me you can do nothing.
6 If anyone does not abide in Me, he is cast out as a branch and is withered; and they gather them and throw them into the fire, and they are burned.
7 If you abide in Me, and My words abide in you, you will be ask what you desire, and it shall be done for you.
8 By this My Father is glorified, that you bear much fruit; so you will be My disciples.

John 15:1-8

CHAPTER FIVE:
God Will Fight Your Battles – and Win

Trust in the Lord… "the battle is not yours, but God's."

> *"Then upon Jahaziel the son of Zechariah…*
> *came the spirit of the LORD in the midst of the*
> *congregation; And he said, Hearken ye, all Judah,*
> *and ye inhabitants of Jerusalem, and thou King*
> *Jehoshaphat, Thus saith the LORD unto you, Be*
> *not afraid nor dismayed by reason of this great*
> *multitude; for the battle is not yours, but God's."*
> II Chronicles 20:14-15

In Jehoshaphat's prayer we discover that the first steps are taken by man toward God, and now we see the beginning of God's answer.

God's message through His prophet to the king and the people of Judah was "I have heard your prayer."

The answer came to Jehoshaphat, and the answer will come to you! As a servant of the living God, I can guarantee you that as you humble yourself before God, the answer will come. It will come with an unmistakable clarity, so that you will know beyond the shadow of a doubt that you have heard from God and that the answer for your deliverance is on the way.

Listen to the assurance that the word of the Lord brought to the heart of the king and his people.

> *"Be not afraid nor dismayed by reason of this*
> *great multitude…"*
> II Chronicles 20:15

"Jehoshaphat, it doesn't matter if there are a hundred or a thousand armies against you, or the whole world is against you because the battle is not yours, but it is God's."

The first thing God does when He comes to answer your prayer is remove every natural limitation.

39

"Jehoshaphat, children of ISRAEL, be not afraid." God doesn't give us the spirit of fear – don't be afraid! Don't be afraid of what the enemy is telling you. Don't be afraid of the circumstance! Don't be afraid of the difficulties! Why should you not be afraid? Why should you not fear when it looks like everything is going wrong? Why shouldn't you be afraid when you can't sleep at night because your mind is being tormented by the devil? Why should you not be afraid? Why? Jahaziel tells you why! Jehoshaphat, the battle is not yours, but it's God's! Go ahead, rejoice!

Now, if you and I were dictating the course of events, at this point we would take the word of the Lord that the battle is not ours and say, "Well, let us go home and be at peace and forget that the enemy ever existed. God is going to fight the battle for us, so apparently there is nothing more for us to do. Thank God that our king prayed such an effective prayer that now the Lord is going to completely intervene for us and victory is ours."

"If God is going to fight the battle, what is there left for us to do but to sit back, relax, and enjoy the sunshine and the fruit of the land?"

Wrong!

It is not time to sit back.

Yes, God is going to fight the battle for you, but that doesn't mean that you are not going to have to face the enemy for yourself.

Now here is where trust comes in. God tells the king and the people through His prophet;

> *To morrow go ye down against them: behold, they come up by the Cliff of Ziz; and ye shall find them at the end of the brook, before the wilderness of Jeruel. Ye shall not need to fight in this battle: set yourselves, stand ye still, and see the salvation of the LORD with you, O Judah and Jerusalem: fear not, nor be dismayed; to morrow go out against them; for the LORD will be with you.*

II Chronicles 20:16-17

Are you ready to say, "Brother Cerullo, I will obey God no matter what!" Jahaziel the prophet told them how to get the victory. He said, "tomorrow" – look in the 16th verse – "go up against them." He said, "I'm going to tell you from where they're going to come. Go up to the cliff of Ziz, and you're going to find them at the end of the brook before the wilderness of Jeruel."

Now, did you know God knows how to put His finger on exactly where you enemy is? You're not going to need to fight in this battle!

What God is saying is that you are going to be face-to-face with the enemy, but you do not need to prepare for war with carnal weapons; you do not need to sharpen your swords and spears of steel because the battle will be fought with spiritual weapons.

Now, you and I would like to view all of our sicknesses, problems, and conflicts from a great distance, but it is God's way to bring us face-to-face with them that we might see the salvation of the Lord.

You see, if God removes us from our problems and then destroys them, we could later believe that just circumstance or chance or a twist of fate made them disappear.

When we are face-to-face with them and see the deliverance of the Lord, then we will know beyond the shadow of a doubt that it was God and not anything else that brought our deliverance.

The Bible tells us that we serve a jealous God who will not share His glory or our worship with another, be it imaginary or real. God wants us to know exactly where the deliverance came from.

In an early step, we talked about being true to our own selves and how this sometimes is really not possible.

When we humble ourselves before God, He will reveal where our enemy really is. We may be going through life blaming our problems on our husband or wife, our children, neighbors, relatives or people with whom we work. We may be blaming it on our place in life and the economic problems that surround us. We may blame it on our parents, but when we humble ourselves before God, we will see exactly where our real enemy is.

I hate the devil and everything he stands for, and every evil curse he has brought upon the world. I realize that he is at the root of most of our problems, but I also realize that he has been used as a scapegoat on many occasions. It is so easy to blame the devil for our problems, when in many cases the responsibility can be laid at our doorstep of laziness and compromise that we have allowed to creep in.

The prophet told the people the exact location of their enemy. *"They come up by the cliff of Ziz; and ye shall find them at the end of the brook before the wilderness of Jeruel"* (II Chronicles 20:16). The location of the enemy is pin-pointed.

In the revelation in my book on the New Anointing, the Spirit of the Lord has taught us how locate our enemy.

Here is another great example. The Holy Spirit did not speak in generalization; He was extremely specific. God did not tell people, "Out in this great wilderness of hills, mountains, and valleys, the enemy that wants to destroy you is hidden, and I want you to go out there and look for them until you find them." That enemy could have kept them in fear for their lives for years, and that would have been worse than death itself. Living in constant fear is a living hell; there is nothing worse except hell itself.

When humility came and the king got off the throne of self, and in essence said, "Lord, you deliver the people because I can't." then the Spirit of God showed them exactly where the enemy was.

You cannot deal with your problem until you know exactly what it is: you have to be ready and willing to face it head on. You can't cover it over and pretend that it isn't there. The element of trust is manifested in your life when you are ready to face your enemy completely unarmed in your own strength.

This is a most vital point. When the Spirit of God shows you exactly where your enemy is, there is a great temptation to do a little of your own warfare on the side. At least, to have something in reserve to protect yourself when you stand face-to-face before your adversary.

God emphasized again to the king and the people,"...fear not, nor be dismayed...for the Lord will be with you."

Trust the Holy Spirit!

When God sends His answer, receive it with a willing and open heart even if it breaks every rule of human understanding. Men today want to put God in a test tube and dissect Him according to the rules of logic.

Let me tell you something. God is not always logical according to our rules of logic because the smartest man that ever lived (apart from Jesus) only "knew in part." The whole picture has never been revealed to man because finite minds are unable to contain it.

There are two words repeated in this Scripture that are important for us to understand. We have mentioned the word "fear," but let us also take a brief view of the meaning of "dismayed."

"Dismay" means to be filled with apprehension and to lose our courage and confidence at the prospect of danger or trouble. You have heard the well-worn story about the day the devil decided to sell every tool, weapon, and device that he possessed; that is, everything with one exception – the wedge of discouragement was not for sale.

If we have absolute trust, there is no room for discouragement. That wedge has no place to get a foothold when our faith and trust are in God. Be ready to have your trust in God put to the test.

God said, "Here is where the enemy is coming. It is not necessary for you to take any weapons to the battle or to fight. Just go and stand in the midst, in the face of the oncoming enemy, and trust Me. I will fight for you."

Right now, before you approach the next step, determine that you are going to put your total trust in the Lord to bring you complete victory for spirit, soul, and body.

CHAPTER SIX:
Faith in Action

Have faith in the Lord and in His servants.

"And they...went forth."

II Chronicles 20:20

God's deliverance requires action on our part – action that is based on faith in the Word that He has sent.

Jehoshaphat could have prayed the greatest prayer ever prayed; he could have humbled himself before God. God could have sent His anointed word through His prophet, but if that was where it stopped, Judah would have been wiped out – eliminated from the face of the earth. Where would that leave you and me today?

Jehoshaphat at that moment was concerned for his life and the lives of his people; but think of the ramifications for generations to come that hung upon his decision to put his faith in action and do what the Lord had commanded.

Jehoshaphat could have said he trusted the Lord, and yet refused to obey Him and go forth under His direction in the hour of testing.

How many times I have said that God never does anything to us, or for us, but always through us. Yes, the battle is not ours; but we must remain the willing instrument in the hand of God that we might "see the salvation of the LORD" (II Chronicles 20:17).

"Wait a minute, Jehoshaphat; wait a minute, ISRAEL. Get up off your knees right now! Now is not praying time; now is not worshipping time. Now it's marching time!"

Jehoshaphat could have believed, but he still had to convince the people to follow him. He stood before the people and declared, "Hear me, O Judah, and ye inhabitants of Jerusalem; Believe in the LORD your God, so shall ye be established; believe his prophets, so shall ye prosper" (II Chronicles 20:20).

Here we can draw a spiritual parallel. We read in the Word

45

of God that "the spirit indeed is willing, but the flesh is weak" (Matthew 26:41). In our hearts we can know that the Word of God is true, but our will must be brought into subjection to the Spirit of God.

Action must be the result!

Judah had to move out of the comfort of Jerusalem in order to confront the enemy face-to-face. If they waited until the enemy reached the gates of the city, it would be too late to act.

Here is another great secret that the revelation of the New Anointing has taught us. We must put the enemy on the run. If we wait until the enemy is at our doorstep, then we are on the defensive and it is harder to gain the victory.

I am a firm believer in meeting and dealing with every problem the moment it rears its ugly head.

Do not live under the cloud of illusion that problems will work themselves out. They will only work you out – out of peace of mind and out of the health, happiness, and prosperity that God wants you to have.

When Jehoshaphat heard about the problem, he immediately took steps to deal with it. He did not wait until the enemy was at the city gates.

Because he dealt with the problem immediately, the Spirit of God was able to lead him on to an offensive venture. He was able to pursue the enemy, not in his own strength, but in the power of the Holy Spirit.

Belief in the Word of God was not enough. It was a foundation upon which to build, but in itself was insufficient.

If you were to stop one thousand people on the streets of your city and take an opinion poll asking the following question, "Do you believe in God?" over 95 percent of them would answer "yes." Yet, that is not enough. The Bible tells us that even the devil and the demons believe and they tremble.

But without faith it is impossible to please him: for
he that cometh to God must believe that he is, and

that he is a rewarder of them that diligently seek him.

Hebrews 11:6

If the Lord had told Judah, "I have heard your prayer and I will take care of everything. You just go back to the regular routine of business as usual," what measure of faith would that have required? Virtually none; they would have done so without a moment's hesitation.

Wait and see the salvation of the Lord.

Every blessing that we receive from God comes to us through faith. We are saved by faith.

For by grace are ye saved through faith; and that not of yourselves: it is the gift of God.

Ephesians 2:8

We are healed by faith; all things come to us by faith. I have seen so many people struggle for faith. Some believe that if they tell themselves often enough that they have faith, that eventually it will become a reality. They will say, "I have faith...I have faith..." from now until their last breath. However, doing that will not increase the measure of your faith.

Early in ministry, God gave me a little saying that has been an eye-opener to tens of thousands of people around the world concerning faith. It is this, "Faith is a fact, but faith is also an act."

Now, if you want a phrase to repeat over and over again, try that one until it really sinks in.

Jehoshaphat could have heard the Word of the Lord through the prophet and said, "We believe." But if they did not do what was told them, they would not be acting on their belief or their faith in the Word.

They could have heard his mighty prophecy and be greatly inspired knowing the Lord had answered the prayer of the king. Yet, if they did not act, it would all be for naught.

I believe in acting on the Word. The greatest revelation

47

in the world is worthless unless it motivates you to do something about it. I am not interested in tickling people's ears. I want to see them so moved by the Holy Spirit that they cannot sit still; they have to get out and put into practice what the Holy Spirit has taught them.

For some time now, God has led us to conduct what we call the School of Ministry in conjunction with every Victory Miracle Crusade. We go into North American cities, sit in a classroom, and teach the people about the revelation called the "New Anointing."

The "New Anointing" revelation is a message of action. You cannot hear it and sit still. It almost compels you to begin to use the spiritual weapons that are placed in your hands. The unique thing about the School of Ministry is that you are immediately given the opportunity to see the principle of spiritual warfare in action.

My Jewish heritage has given me the attitude that I am not interested in how high-sounding something may be. What I want to know is, does it really work?

As the people come out of the day session of the School of Ministry, they are brought into the evening crusade rallies and come face-to-face with every type of sickness, disease, and demonic power.

At these rallies, people can begin to use the weapons of spiritual warfare that Christ has given his church. They can use the truths they have learned come to pass right before their eyes; in many cases because they have exercised the faith God placed in their hearts.

Faith is action! Faith is positive!

> *For he that wavereth is like a wave of the sea driven with the wind and tossed. For let not that man think that he shall receive any thing of the Lord.*
>
> James 1:6-7

Now, I am a man who thanks God for what we receive in the natural. I thank God for doctors. However, isn't it interesting; one day you're told to take a certain medication and after you have taken it for fifteen years the doctor tells you, "Oh, you've been taking the wrong thing. This drug will cause this disease. In fact, it may kill you." What am I trying to say? They are practicing physicians. They practice on you.

Now, I am not being critical. There is nothing wrong with man learning from experience and advances in science. However, I hope it will put the weakness and frailty of man into perspective!

One day I was sitting in the kitchen of my home in San Diego, California. Suddenly, I felt a hand touch my shoulder. I turned around to look and nobody was there. Immediately, God's presence engulfed me and He spoke. He said, "Son, tell My people everything that can be shaken will be shaken. Tell them to fix their faith on that which cannot be shaken."

When you fix your faith on what cannot be shaken, no theologian can destroy your position. No one can come along with a passing doctrine and sway you this way or that, bringing you into absolute confusion!

Receive this into your spirit; there is only one power in the world that cannot be shaken. It is not the power of the government. It is not the power of the human minds. It is the power of the Word of the living God.

> *In the beginning was the Word, and Word was with God and the Word was God...All things were made by him; and without him was not anything made that was made.*
>
> John: 1,3

Put these two words into your spirit:

ONE – infallible, meaning "no margin for error."

TWO – impregnable, meaning "impossible to be taken by assault."

Man has never, nor will ever achieve the position where he is without margin for error. Man is not infallible.

But, the Word of God is infallible. That means His Word

will never fail you. The Word of God makes you impregnable. This means the devil can throw anything and everything at you, but you cannot be shaken because your faith has been fixed on that which will never fail you!

When you hear somebody say that it is not God's will for them to be well, you know that they have bought one of the devil's biggest lies. Do not ever let anyone tell you that it is God's will for you to be sick or afflicted.

I have heard people go so far as to believe they are suffering their affliction for Christ. This is worst lie yet. Such a message implies that Christ's death and resurrection was not enough. You would have to complete the work He has already done for you.

Did Jehoshaphat waver at the command of God? Did he sit down and say, "Now I wonder if it really is the will of God to deliver Judah from his enemies? Maybe we ought to really consider this, because we certainly don't want to go out and defeat the enemy if it is not God's will."

Sound silly? Yes, but no more silly than a born-again, spirit-filled Christian saying, "I wonder if it really is the will of God for me to have victory over this sin in my life? I wonder if it really is the will of God to save my husband, to save my wife, or to bring back my wayward, prodigal son or daughter?"

It is not only important to believe God, but Jehoshaphat said to the people that they must believe God's servants as well; "So shall ye prosper."

Upon Jahaziel, the son of Zechariah, came the Spirit of Prophecy. He told them what to do. They believed it and they acted upon it.

Today, if someone gives a message in prophecy relative to people and circumstances, this person might be branded as a religious fanatic. If that is being a fanatic, I want to be used of God as one!

We need more Jahaziels in our world today. You can read this message, begin to reason the various steps in your mind, and try to apply human understanding. I am sure that you can sit down and pick apart this point or that, but where will it get you?

On the other hand, you can say, "Lord, I believe that you have put this in my hand. Although I may not fully comprehend every point, I am going to do just what this prophet of God has said and I am going to have the victory in Jesus' Name."

Are you ready for the final step?

This is the capstone...don't miss it...you have gone too far to stop now!

Faith is the Victory! Oh, glorious Victory – that overcomes the world.

CHAPTER SEVEN:
Praise the Lord for the Victory

And when he had consulted with the people, he appointed singers unto the LORD, and that should praise the beauty of holiness, as they went out before the army, and to say, Praise the LORD; for his mercy endureth for ever.

II Chronicles 20:21

You've surrendered yourself. You've humbled yourself before God! You have come before Him and recognized that there was nothing you could do to fight this battle! God said, "You don't have to fight it because it's not yours!" God is fighting the battle!

Do you want me to prove it? Do you want me to go all the way back to Genesis?

This battle never was between man and the devil. It has always been between God and the devil, and always will be!

Are you ready for victory? Better get ready! Get your running shoes on! You are not going to need to fight in this battle. Stand tall, stand still, and see the salvation of the Lord your God!

Are you ready to learn what the victory is? Here it is. If God is fighting the battle, then why do you try to get involved? Do you know what God told the people in Genesis? He said, "Put down your sword. You don't need your sword." God was talking about our natural weapons. He calls you to use your spiritual shield and sword, but you do not need to use your *natural* sword.

God asks, "Do you know how you are going to receive victory?" Then, He answers, "You are going to go look at the enemy." He tells the people to do what? *Stand still* and *look*. When does the victory come? When they looked in the face of the enemy, dropped their natural weapons, lifted up their voices, and shouted praises unto God! When they shouted, praised, and sang, God opened the heavens!

When they began to shout, and praise...then the heavens opened.

Next, God sent ambushes upon His people's enemies. God destroyed the enemy when they began to praise Him for their victory!

Praise the Lord for victory in *your* circumstances and over every attack of the enemy. God has fought the battle for you, and Jesus has won the victory for you!

It is easy to praise God after the fact, but that is not the point of this message. Immediately after they had received the Word of the Lord from the Prophet Jahaziel, Jehoshaphat bowed; he put his heart and soul into worshiping God.

When the king set the example (v. 18), the Bible tells us that all of Judah and the inhabitants of Jerusalem followed suit.

What a picture! We may look at this group as a bunch of primitive people. However, let me tell you they had as much or more protocol, ritual, and form than we can imagine.

Let your imagination take hold of you for a moment. Can you conceive of the spiritual explosion that could take place in this nation if every minister on next Sunday morning faced their congregation and declared that the order of service was going to be different? Would the printed program include each person bowing their heads in worship and praise to thank God for delivering our nation from its present turmoil?

No. Do you know why this is unlikely to happen soon?

The reason this has not taken place is because the church does not really believe it is facing a crisis. It has not been given the news that the enemy has amassed his strength and is about to attack. In many cases, the message has come, but has been disregarded and was even considered fanatical.

In Revelation, the present-day church says, "I am rich and increased with goods, and have need of nothing (Revelation 3:17). The Holy Spirit testifies that the church's real spiritual picture is "naked" and "blind" during these end times.

Jehoshaphat bowed and worshipped the Lord, and the people worshipped with him. They thanked the Lord for the word that He had given. They did not complain that they had to leave their homes to meet their enemies. They also did not complain that they might miss a supper meal or a day's pay on the job.

Instead, the people began to thank him for their victory when asked to do what seemed an impossible task. God asked them to go forth and meet their enemies, but without all of the regular preparation for war. God commanded them to not only to go meet their enemies, but told them to "stand still and see the salvation of the Lord." God commanded them to take faith-filled action by going forth, despite being physically prepared and knowing what would happen on the battle line. God, however, knew "the battle was not theirs, but His."

As the king and all of Judah were on their faces praising and worshipping God, we read "the priests rose up to praise the LORD God of ISRAEL with a loud voice on high" (II Chronicles 20:19). It sounds like they were getting a little emotional.

You may be thinking, "Do you mean to say that shouting and praising the Lord did not begin back on Azusa Street in 1904? You mean that loud praise is not exclusive only with Pentecostals?"

No. When you know the answer has come from the Lord, there is good reason to get excited. I can tell you that at this moment Judah was excited! Certain doom had been changed into certain victory! They had received God's word, and they were expressing their feelings of joy and happiness!

Praise the Lord as He answers you! You do not need to wait until the deliverance is accomplished. In fact, deliverance may not come until you praise the Lord for the Victory!

Immediately after they had heard from the Lord, the people entered into a period of praise. Judah was strengthened to stand up and go out into the wilderness to face their enemies.

The Bible says, "The joy of the LORD is your strength" (Nehemiah 8:10). This is such a simple yet profound statement of fact. Do not try to go out and face your enemy until you have the joy of the Lord in your heart. This strength of joy will come into your heart as you begin by faith to praise and worship the Lord.

In the natural, Judah had nothing for which to praise the Lord concerning their deliverance from their enemies. Their enemies were a united front against the king and the people of Judah and were marching toward them as they waited in Jerusalem.

After a day of prayer and praise before the Lord, the nation was ready to march. Yes, the *whole* nation was ready. There was no paid, professional army that was designated to meet their enemies. The *entire* nation was ready and willing to face the battle together.

The Bible tell us the people of Judah rose up early (II Chronicles 20:20). There is a tremendous lesson in faith in their early morning discipline. They gathered together in the wilderness, but before they met their enemies, the king halted their march. Why did he stop them? Do you think it was because he wanted to put the strongest men out front and the weaker, more vulnerable women and children behind? Is that what he did?

No! Instead, the king found those with the best and strongest voices. These chosen were given the huge responsibility to lead the people in praise and worship as they marched forward to face their enemies.

Are you thinking, "What a strange leader!"?

Why didn't he find the most accurate marksman, or the one with the best armor? This was not a physical battle. It was a spiritual one. However, that did not mean that God did not want them to do anything to take action. The people's "weapon" of battle was praising God. The entire nation of Judah began to praise the Lord in the face of battle.

What happened as a result of this unusual strategy?

The Bible says, "And when they began to sing and praise, the LORD set ambushments against the children of Ammon, Moab, and Mount Seir, which were come against Judah; and they were smitten" (see II Chronicles 20:22).

The New Living Translation of this verse says, "The moment they began to praise the Lord, their enemy was defeated!" God had honored the people's faith as they obeyed the king to praise and worship God before they knew the outcome.

When ISRAEL began to praise the Lord, their enemies turned on each other and completely destroyed one another. The enemy destroyed itself.

When you praise and worship God from the depths of an honest and sincere heart, it is as if you are pushing a self-destruct button for everything that opposes you – whether your opposition is sickness, emotional problems, or financial problems.

Do you want to fight your own battles, winning one here and losing two there? Do you always want to lose ground – things always getting worse and seldom getting better? Or, would you rather follow God's formula and be able to stand back and see the deliverance of the Lord?

> *And when Judah came toward the watchtower in the wilderness, they looked unto the multitude and, behold, they were dead bodies fallen to the earth, and none escaped.*
>
> II Chronicles 20:24

That Scripture is so beautiful! The multitude of enemies ended up as dead bodies. None had escaped!

Jehoshaphat had not known *how* the victory was going to come. He did not have any clue *how* God was going to work. Yet, despite his lack of knowing, he stood in the midst of the enemy, faced the battle line, and praised God for the victory – even before he saw it come to pass.

Let me tell you something. It is one thing to simply decide to manage, deal with or just get through a crisis. But, it is quite another to make a choice and take action to stand face-to-face against the devil – especially if you have cancer, your children are on drugs, or your home is breaking up. When you stand face-to-face with the enemy you must believe in faith the Word of God and the word of the prophet!

The people of ISRAEL did not know how God was going to deliver and bring them into victory. Neither do you know *how* God will do the same for you. So, why should you care how He brings you deliverance and victory – or *how* He will heal the cancer?

Although you may not know *how* or when your personal victory will happen, you do know this truth according to the Word of God – it will happen!

You *can* praise God *in the midst* of the situation before the face of the enemy.

You *can* praise God *while you are facing* the battle and can see your adversary attacking your soul, your home or your body.

Praise God for the victory!

Yes, before – even during – the raging of the battle.

Praise Him for the victory!

Praise Him – you will overcome!

Praise Him in spite of the enemy! No matter how hard the enemy tries to battle your family, or your body – he is a defeated foe.

Praise God for the victory!

Before I write the concluding paragraph, I feel led by the Holy Spirit to ask you to do this:

1. Right now, take pen in your hand. Go sit at your living or dining room table. Write down on the prayer request page in the back of this book all your burdens, problems, sicknesses, and any needs you may have.

2. As you are doing this, visualize me sitting next to you at the table. You are unreservedly pouring out your needs to me – a servant of the Lord. You can say aloud "Brother Cerullo, I need you to please pray with me about this need."

Remember – FAITH IS A FACT, BUT FAITH IS ALSO AN ACT.

Now, I want you to do two things with your prayer request:

1. First, finish reading the last several paragraphs of this book with your list of written needs held alongside the book as you read. Go through the seven keys to personal victory you'll find in the paragraphs that follow one-by-one. Pray and meditate about your needs written out on paper. Have the last several paragraphs of this book by your side to guide you.

2. Then, take this step of faith. Send me the needs you have written out. Do it now. Don't delay one moment. Tell me, "Brother Cerullo, I have taken this particular problem, this family need, this sickness to God through these seven steps, and now I praise Him for it even before I see it come to pass."

I will personally pray for your needs through intercessory prayer, then place your prayer request on the altar in our chapel for praise and victory. Stop and send your request right now – while the witness of the Holy Spirit is with you. I can feel the Holy Spirit witnessing to your heart right now.

NOW YOU ARE READY FOR THE FINAL PARAGRAPHS?

God's victory is complete – He never does it halfway. If you have followed His formula revealed throughout this book, *Keys to Walking in Personal Victory: The Battle Is Not Yours, but God's!,* your victory will be complete.

Take these key words and memorize them:
Recognize
Remember
Stand
Humble
Trust
Faith
Praise

1. **Recognize** – Jehoshaphat recognized the power and the authority of the God he was serving.

59

2. **Remember** – He then remembered the acts of deliverance that God had already accomplished for His people.

3. **Stand** – He then affirmed his position to stand completely on the Word of God. He was standing in the presence of the Lord and before the House of the Lord where the Word of God resided.

4. **Humble** – Next, Jehoshaphat humbled himself before the mighty hand of God and acknowledged his utter dependence upon God for deliverance.

5. **Trust** – He then put his trust in the Lord. The Lord answered his prayer and gave the directives on how the victory was to be achieved.

6. **Faith** – He showed his faith in God's Word, not only with a verbal declaration, but he put his faith in action as he marched toward his enemies. He did not depend on the army of flesh (humans), but solely on the Lord.

7. **Praise** – Finally, Jehoshaphat led the people to praise and worship the Lord before the answer came for their deliverance and victory. Then, the people went forth to meet their enemies.

Every one of these keys are applicable to every problem of life, whether it be physical or spiritual. I do not believe there is anyone who cannot apply these keys one-at-a-time and come into victory.

These *Keys for Walking in Personal Victory* were given to me by God. They are based on His Word and were revealed to me as I was on my knees in prayer!

The Word of God will not fail. Act on what you *now* believe. Walk in new faith. Right now, receive God's Victory!

"SO THE REALM OF JEHOSHAPHAT WAS QUIET: FOR HIS GOD GAVE HIM REST ROUND ABOUT" (II Chronicles 20:30).

Remember: God has no defeats planned for you. Only victory through Jesus Christ, His Son!

...and God gave me a vision!

There is a greater anointing upon me now than ever before to pray for your needs.

Never before, in my more than 58 years of frontline ministry have I carried a deeper burden for the Body of Christ than I do now. I have prayed, fasted, interceded, agonized, and fought spiritual warfare against satanic powers...

...and God gave me a vision!

A vision of Jesus Christ, our Great High Priest, praying for all your needs.

God said, *"Place the needs of my people upon the altar before My Presence. Jesus is praying for all their needs to be met."*

Every need, every disease, every family problem, every circumstance... God wants me to lift your need for Jesus to pray for you. Do not delay. Write all your needs on the following page and mail it to me today!

For prayer call:

1-858-HELPLINE
1-858-435-7546

Brother Cerullo,

Please place these requests on the Miracle Prayer Altar and pray for these needs:

_____

_____

_____

_____

_____

_____

❑ Enclosed is my love gift of $(£)_____ to help you win souls and to support this worldwide ministry.

❑ Please tell me how I can become a God's Victorious Army member...to help you reach the nations of the world and receive even more anointed teaching on a monthly basis!

Name _____

Address _____

City _____ State or Province _____

Postal Code _____ Phone Number ( ) _____

E-mail _____

Fax _____

Mail today to:

MORRIS CERULLO WORLD EVANGELISM
San Diego: P.O. Box 85277 • San Diego, CA 92186
Canada: P.O. Box 3600 • Concord, Ontario L4K 1B6
U.K.: P.O. Box 277 • Hemel Hempstead, Herts HP2 7DH
Web site: www.mcwe.com• E-mail: morriscerullo@mcwe.com

For prayer, call: 1-858-HELPLINE

HELPLINE FAX: 1-858-427-0555

HELPLINE e-mail: helpline@mcwe.com

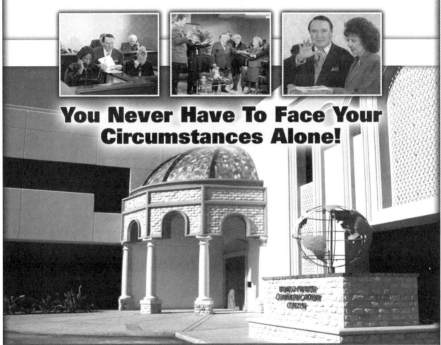